CAROL BURNETT

What I Want to Be
WHEN I GROW UP

CREATED BY

George Mendoza and Sheldon Secunda

PHOTOGRAPHY BY

Sheldon Secunda

SIMON AND SCHUSTER · NEW YORK

Published by Simon and Schuster
Rockefeller Center, 630 Fifth Avenue
New York, New York 10020
Designed by Eve Metz
Manufactured in the United States of America
By Rand McNally & Company, Skokie, Ill.

1   2   3   4   5   6   7   8   9   10

Library of Congress Cataloging in Publication Data
Burnett, Carol
      What I want to be when I grow up.

      1. Burnett, Carol—Portraits, caricatures, etc.   2. Children's writings, American.   3. Children's art.   I. Mendoza, George, joint author.   II. Secunda, Sheldon, joint author.   III. Title.
PN2287.B85A35   790.2′092′4   75-22103
ISBN 0-671-22159-0

Many children contributed poems and drawings, some of which appear in this book. Though we couldn't use all the material submitted, we are grateful for everyone's participation.

"Well, hello there, little girl. And what do you want to be when you grow up?"

I used to retort "An adult," but secretly I longed to be Brenda Starr, the gorgeous red-headed ace reporter in the Sunday comics who was having an ill-fated romance with the mysterious Basil St. John who wore a black patch over his eye and could never marry Brenda because of something dreadful in his past....

As I matured, naturally I became more practical. I wanted to be Betty Grable. But it was in college that I began to discover what I really wanted to be. I remember we were doing an original play for the student body of UCLA and I dressed up as a hillbilly— blackened tooth, freckles…the works—and said the first line: "I'm back." The audience howled (you had to have been there).

It was an extraordinary feeling, totally exhilarating—and then it hit me! What I really wanted to be was a comedienne.

Now, if you asked anyone at that time if a woman could succeed as a comedienne with her own weekly TV variety show and play to an audience of 25 million families, the answer was no. Emphatically no!

But—and here's the trick—I didn't ask anyone else. I did it myself because I wanted to do it, even if it was the most unlikely, outrageous and insane thing to do. I worked hard—and it worked!

Now we live in Betty Grable's former house, and when my children come to me and ask me what they can be when they grow up, I tell them they can be anything they like. A woman can be a detective, a magician, an explorer; a man can be a cook, a concert pianist, a mountain climber. In this book, I've tried to put together all the choices of professions I could think of; I also asked a bunch of kids to think with me, and their ideas are included too. The most important thing is to love what you do.

I never stopped fantasizing, and my dreams finally came true. My job gives me the chance to be anyone I want to be—from Joan Crawford to Groucho Marx to Mae West to Bugs Bunny, and I love it! It's nice being an adult, but it's great to still feel like a kid.

Carol Burnett

SKINDIVER

I Want to be a Veterinarian because I Love animals.

Ruthanne Secunda

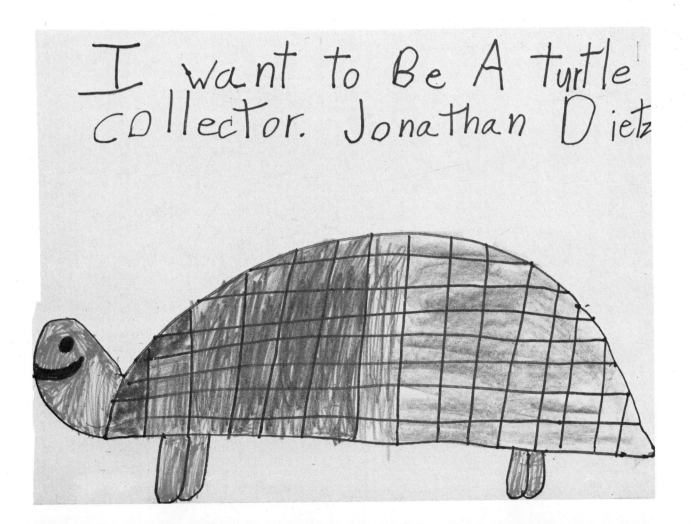

I want to Be A turtle collector. Jonathan Dietz

SHOEMAKER

ROCK SINGER

dancer

Jackie Snepter

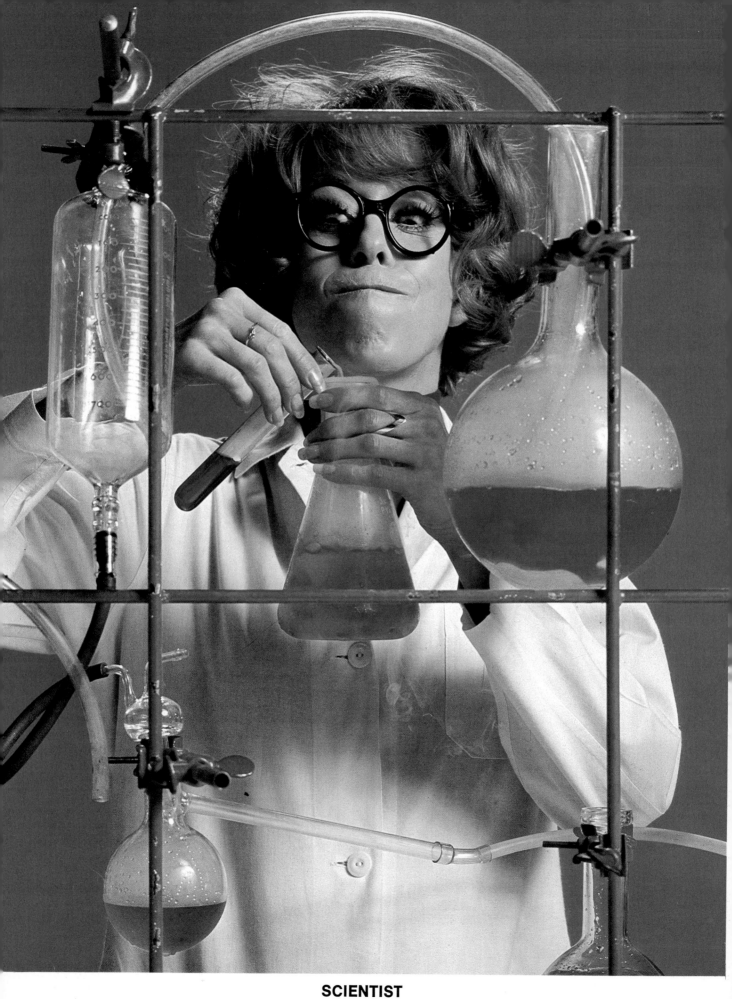

SCIENTIST

ANGLER

PILOT

Julie McConnell

      What I Want to Be when
I grow up!

A pilot

      I love flying and I love
the sky. Because it goes on
forever and nothing cages you
in And when I am in a
plane I feel like getting
out and jumping on the
puffy white clouds

PET STORE OWNER

LEPIDOPTERIST

FIREFIGHTER

KARATE INSTRUCTOR

CONSTRUCTION WORKER

TENNIS PLAYER

BOAT BUILDER

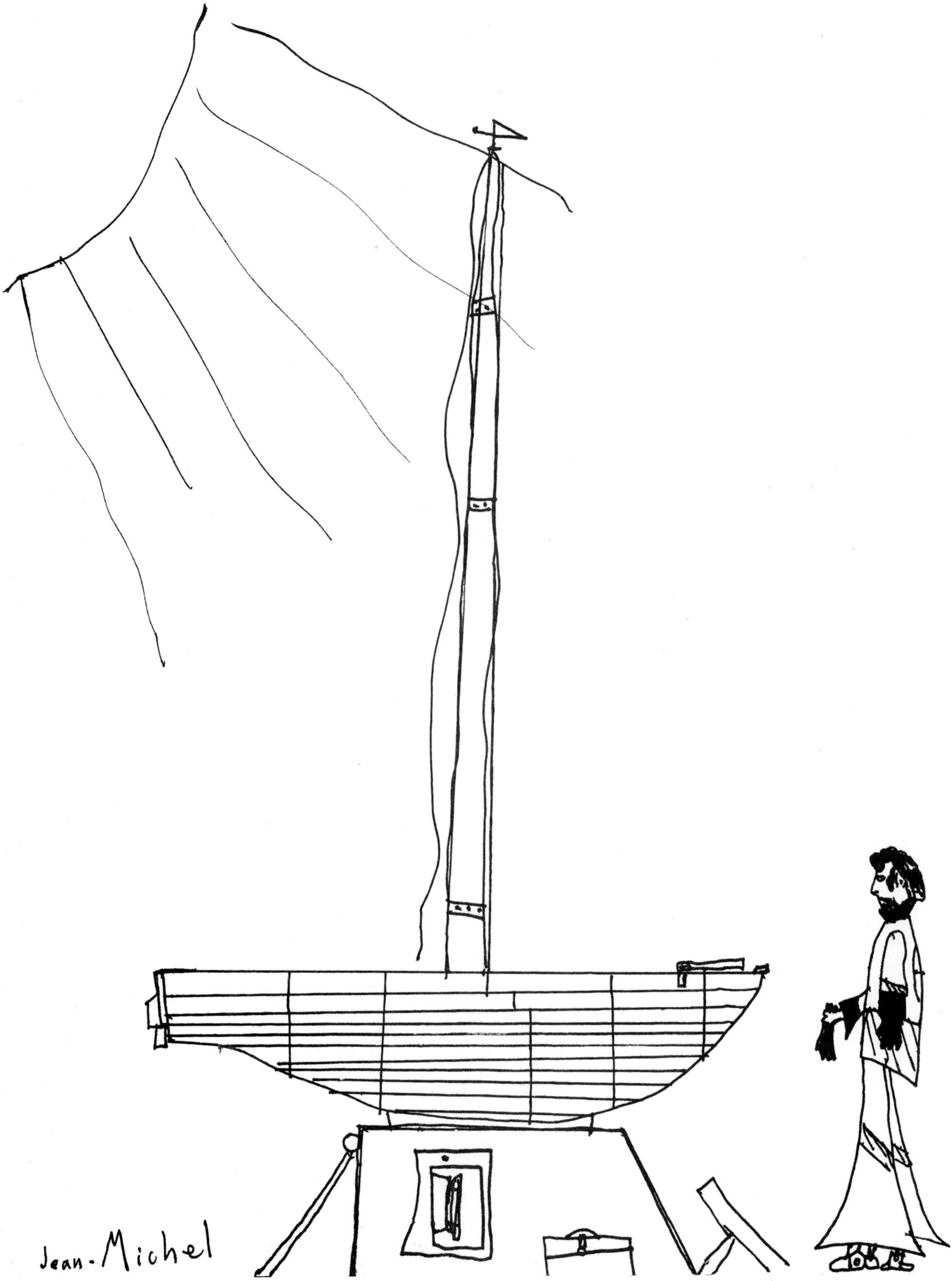

Jean-Michel

Ricki Stern   a olympic skier

SHOE SALESMAN   Matthew Snyder

DANCER

POLICE OFFICER

FORTUNE-TELLER

FORESTER

PHOTOGRAPHER

MINER

Danny Smith age 8

When I grow up I want to be a baseball player. I want play first base. I want to play with San Diego Padres.

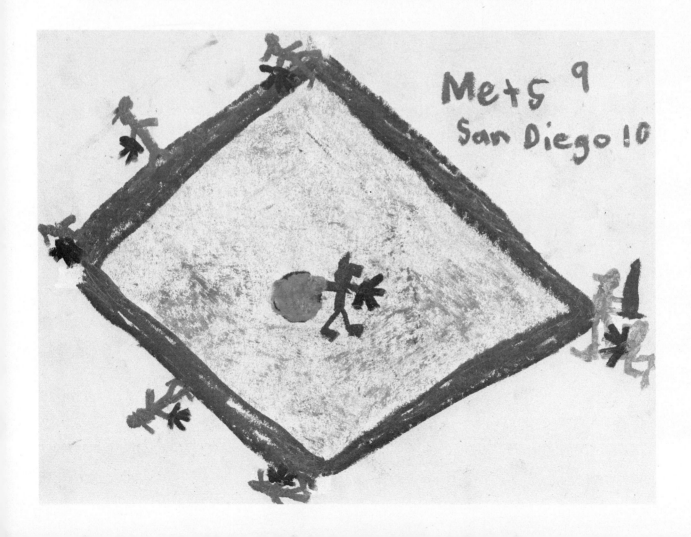

Mets 9
San Diego 10

Patrick N.Z Rona   SPORTSCARS RACER

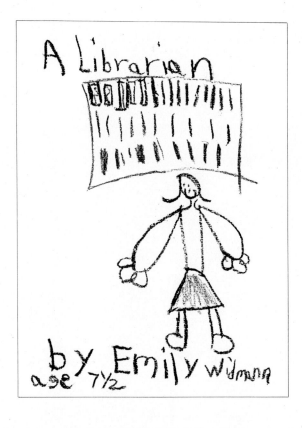

A Librarian

by Emily Widmana
age 7½

VETERINARIAN

GOLFER

MOVIE STAR

DETECTIVE

CHESS PLAYER

Ashley A

clown

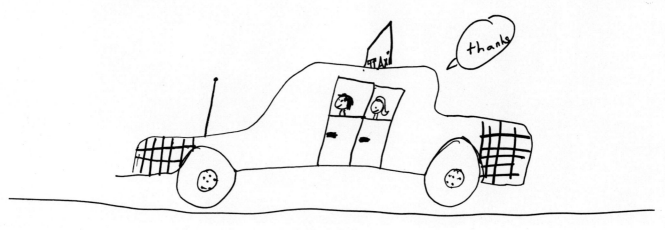

CAB DRIVER

FARMER

FOOTBALL PLAYER

TRAPEZE ARTIST

PSYCHIATRIST

TV REPAIRER

ACCOUNTANT

WEIGHT LIFTER

LETTER CARRIER

WhEn I grow up I want.
To BE an ArTist.

when I grow up I want to be a singer.

Anf Rodriguez

I want to be a ballerina

CARPENTER

CAB DRIVER

ACROBAT

ASTRONAUT

PIZZA MAKER

Philip Cavalier 3y

I I want to be a reverend
When I grow up I want
to be a reverend. I want
to be a reverend and serve
God on the alter of heaven.
I'll feel so secure. I
will wear a black vestment,
will be a servent to God.

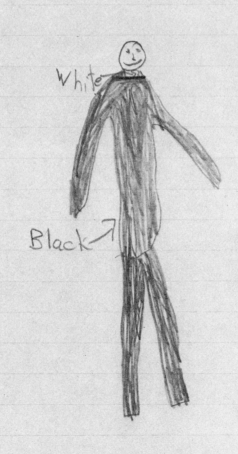

White

Black →

I Would Like to Be a Teacher.

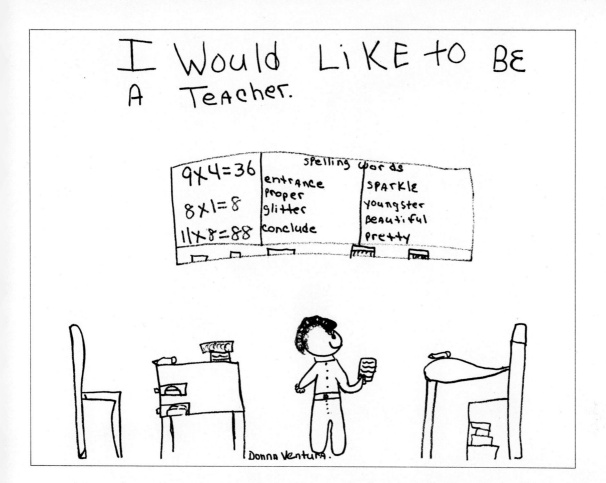

SCUBA DIVER

MODEL

DOCTOR

D. J.

WRITER

Today I am getting my writers license my first book will be How to have fun don't try to get a job. I do hope you like it. by writer Mike Gelb 203

LIFEGUARD

CYCLIST

MAGICIAN

SEA CAPTAIN

TELEPHONE LINEMAN

When I grow up I would like to be a pediatrician because I love babies and like helping people.

BASEBALL PLAYER

COMIC

SOMEDAY I MIGHT EVEN BE PRESIDENT.

If you want to know the actual truth, I'm really all grown-up now. But <u>you</u> still have the opportunity to become what you want to become. And whatever you become, the most important thing is ... <u>be yourself</u>.